BULLIES

Are a Pain in the Brain

Written and illustrated by
Trevor Romain

Edited by Elizabeth Verdick

free spirit
PUBLISHING®

Works
for kids-

Library of Congress Cataloging-in-Publication Data
Romain, Trevor.
    Bullies are a pain in the brain / written and illustrated by Trevor Romain; edited by Elizabeth Verdick.
       p.   cm.
    Includes bibliographical references.
    Summary: A serious yet humorous guide to dealing with bullies.
    ISBN 1-57542-023-6
    1. Bullying—Juvenile humor. [1. Bullying. 2. Bullies.]
I. Verdick, Elizabeth. II. Title.
  BF637.B85R66   1997
  302.3'4—dc21   97-11677
                                           CIP
                                           AC

Cover art/design by Trevor Romain

Thanks to the National Crime Prevention Council for use of the McGruff the Crime Dog art on page 35.

10 9 8 7 6 5 4 3 2

Printed in the United States of America

Free Spirit Publishing Inc.
400 First Avenue North, Suite 616
Minneapolis, MN 55401
(612) 338-2068
help4kids@freespirit.com
www.freespirit.com

Dedication

For Lindsey Gothard, who simply refuses to let childhood cancer bully her.

In memory of Dr. Lee Willerman, a great man who always had faith in me.

Acknowledgments

Sincere thanks to my superb editor Elizabeth Verdick, who worked exceptionally hard on this book. Many thanks to Judy Galbraith and all at Free Spirit for creating and maintaining an incredible publishing company that truly cares about enriching children's lives.

Special thanks to Dr. Allan L. Beane, Professor, College of Education, Murray State University in Murray, Kentucky, for his expertise and his caring, helpful comments.

Contents

Do You Have a Bully Problem?

The alarm clock buzzes and you slowly crawl out of bed. Another school day, and you're miserable. For the past few weeks, a kid in your class has been picking on you, pushing you when the teacher isn't looking, calling you "Dog Breath" (or worse), making you do embarrassing things, and generally getting on your nerves. You didn't do anything to provoke this behavior, and you're wondering why the bully has chosen *you* for a target. You get your lunch money from your mom and hide it in your shoe, hoping that the bully won't try to take your money today. Then you go to wait for the school bus. When it pulls up, you see the bully staring out at you from the back of the bus with a mean grin. "Uh-oh," you think. "How am I supposed to handle this today?"

Does any of this sound familiar?

If you're trying to cope with a bully problem, here's the first thing you need to know:

You're not alone.

Everyone has been bullied at some point. Other kids in your school or neighborhood are probably dealing with bully problems similar to yours. The trouble is, most people keep bully problems a secret. They feel ashamed or scared to talk about what's really happening. They think that if they ignore the situation, it will go away. (It won't.)

Here's the second thing you need to know about your bully problem:

It's not your fault.

You're not doing the bullying. Someone else is. You didn't ask to be bullied. Someone else decided to bully you. Was it something you did? Something you said? Is it because of how you look or where you live or what you wear or any other reason you can possibly think of? (Nope.)

What is a bully, anyway? Here's how *Webster's Dictionary* defines one:

> "A blustering, browbeating person; especially one who is habitually cruel to others."

In other words: Bullies are people with problems. They like to hurt and frighten people they see as smaller or weaker. Experts tell us that bullies like to be in control. By controlling you, a bully feels strong and superior. And you feel puny, afraid—and angry.

BULLIES ARE A PAIN IN THE BRAIN!

Bullies are found everywhere—in small communities, towns, big cities, playgrounds, neighborhoods, malls, parks, on the streets, and anywhere else people gather. Most of all, bullies are found in schools. You may have one sitting right next to you in class.

Bullies come in all shapes and sizes. Boys can be bullies, and so can girls. Adults can be bullies, too. Bullies have been around for centuries. In fact, they've been bothering, pestering, hurting, and troubling people for too long. The good news is, bullies can be stopped.

This book will help you to understand why some people are bullies and how you can deal with them. You'll read about becoming "Bully-Proof," stopping bullies from hurting others, and getting help in dangerous situations. If you're the one doing the bullying, this book can also help you. You'll see that you *can* get along with others, and feel good about yourself, without making other people's lives a complete misery. And you can also learn to deal with the bullies in *your* life.

Young people have a right to feel safe, secure, and protected at school and in their communities. If you don't feel safe, reading this book can be the first step toward changing that.

Quick Quiz

Which of these words describe bullies?

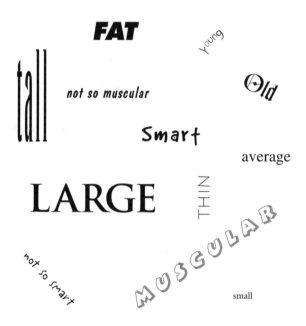

The answer? All of the above!

Why Bullies Are Such a Pain

Bullies can be big or little, tall or short, husky or skinny, brainy or dumb. You can't always identify bullies by their looks. But there's one thing bullies have in common: They like to be in charge. The more they drain the self-esteem of others, the better they feel.

You might even say that bullies are Self-Esteem Vampires.

Bullies harm people in many different ways—physically, mentally, and emotionally. These are the things bullies do best: hit, punch, kick, tease, push, pull, pester, brag, taunt, harass, play mind games, frighten, heckle, insult, annoy, gossip, bother, hurt, threaten, torment, ridicule, trip, pinch, act violent, and intimidate.

Imagine listing those "skills" on your resume when you're looking for a job. Picture a bully at a job interview:

Boss: "Did you excel at anything while in school?"
Bully: "Er . . . yes, Sir, I *did* excel at something in school. I was really good at punching other people out. In fact, I was the best!"

Here's what bullies aren't so good at: making friends, being kind, caring about people, sharing, and getting along with others. Often, bullies come from homes where the parents yell a lot or use physical force to make their kids behave. As a result, bullies have a lot of anger inside them.

What do bullies do with their anger? They take it out on the people (or pets) around them. Bullies choose their victims *verrrry* carefully. Most bullies pick on those who aren't likely to defend themselves.

Give bullies lots of space, because they lose their temper quickly. If you can smell a bully's breath, you're too close! Being near a bully when she loses her temper is like peering into a water fountain when someone turns it on. **LOOK OUT!**

What You Can Do About Bullies

Bullies go after people who appear anxious, sensitive, quiet, or cautious. Like ants are attracted to candy, bullies are drawn to people who are somewhat shy. They might also pick on those who are younger or physically smaller.

So, what's your best defense? A disguise, you say . . . ?

*N*o, you don't have to wear a disguise or change who you are, just because a bully has decided to bother you. Instead, work on appearing more sure of yourself. Stand up straight, look people in the eye, talk with a firm voice, and hold your head high. If you *act* more confident, you'll soon start to *feel* more confident.

Before:

After:

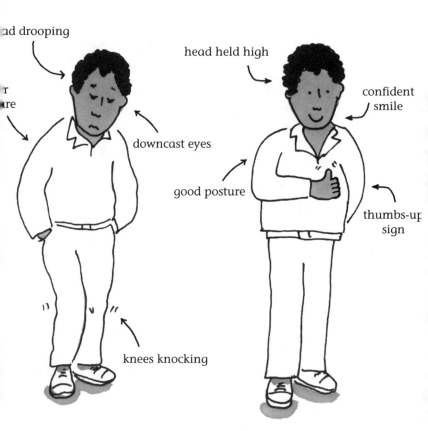

ad drooping

r
re

downcast eyes

knees knocking

head held high

confident
smile

good posture

thumbs-up
sign

Bullies can be very competitive. They hate to lose at sports, games, races—or *anything*. To make sure they win, some bullies play dirty. They cheat, or they beat up anyone who stands in their way.

Some bullies demand "payment" from their victims: "Gimme your lunch money or else." "Let me cheat off your test or I'll hurt you." "Cool sneakers—hand 'em over!" They get rich quick from taking other people's belongings. Sometimes they even destroy or vandalize other people's property.

Bullies think they've hit the jackpot when they make you cry. Don't reward a bully with tears. Instead, stay as calm as you can and walk away with confidence.

Bullies love power. The more they get, the more they want. If messing with electricity wasn't so dangerous, bullies would probably put their fingers into light sockets to get even *more* power.

*T*here *is* one thing worse than a bully—a group of bullies. What do you call a group of bullies? A gang. Gangs are dangerous. Because the gang members outnumber you, they can be even more intimidating. The safest thing to do is *avoid gangs altogether.* Gang members may try to persuade you to join them. Don't believe that you'll be more cool, popular, or tough by belonging to a gang. Many gang members end up in jail, in the hospital, or dead.

The sign held by the figure reads:

NEW RECRUITS
WANTED.
GREAT BENEFITS.

Some gangs carry weapons, making them even more dangerous. What should you do if you see someone who has a gun or knife? Leave the area quickly and quietly. Don't threaten, ignore, attack, or provoke the person. Once you're in a safe place, immediately tell an adult about the weapon. You can tell a parent, teacher, school counselor, your principal, or a police officer.

If bullies or a gang are targeting you, take the long way home.

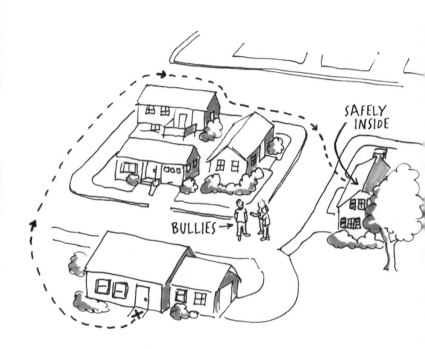

SAFELY INSIDE

BULLIES →

Take the **EXTRA** long way home, if necessary.*

*Even better, find a friend to walk home with. Or ask your
 parents to come pick you up.

If they still come after you, **RUN!** (You might look a bit foolish running down the street like a maniac, but you will look *alive.*)

RUN home, if it's close enough to run to. **RUN** to a group of people, if there's one nearby. **RUN** to a McGruff house or other block parent program. These are safe places especially for kids who are bullied, followed, or hurt while walking in a neighborhood. Find out if there's a block parent program in your neighborhood. Learn where it is. If your neighborhood doesn't have one, tell your parents. Ask if they can work with your neighbors or police department to start one.

A McGruff house will have a picture of McGruff the Crime Dog with the words "McGruff house" in a window or on a door.

Bullies can be a real pain, because they often see another person's success as their own failure. Then they become jealous and angry, and they want to hurt the person who's succeeding. Duh! If these bullies would stop and think for a moment, they might realize that *they* are responsible for what happens in their life. (Did I say *responsible?* Sorry! I forgot that you can't say "bullies" and "responsible" in the same sentence. The two just don't go together.)

Sometimes a bully or a group of bullies will make your life miserable by:

- threatening or insulting you,
- holding you down,
- making jokes about you,
- purposely ignoring you in a mean way,
- giving you dirty looks,
- calling you names,
- making unfriendly gestures, and/or
- spreading rumors about you.

You probably feel scared, sad, angry, alone, and frustrated when you're being bullied. That's exactly how the bully *wants* you to feel! Don't let a bully take away your self-esteem. Find your strengths and achieve your goals. That way, no matter how hard the bully tries to tear down your self-esteem, you'll keep believing in yourself. You'll be Bully-Proof!

Believe it or not, people can actually bully *themselves*. They do this by telling themselves, "I'm no good," or "I'm stupid," or "I can't do anything right." They make *themselves* feel scared, sad, angry, alone, and frustrated.

If you're bullying yourself, **CUT IT OUT.** Start telling yourself, "I'm a strong person," "I'm smart," "I can do it." If there's something you want to achieve, and you really try, you'll probably succeed. (Even if you don't, you'll feel good that you gave it your best shot.)

Make friends—lots of them! Bullies can't stand groups of happy, smiling, friendly people.

Have you ever wondered what friends are *really* for (besides being homework helpers, frog-hunting partners, secret keepers, and trading-card swappers)? Here's what: Friends are for sticking by you in tough times. Tell your friends if you're being bullied. A bully is less likely to approach you if you're surrounded by your buddies. Plus your friends could even say to the bully, "We don't like the way you treat our friend," or, "We don't like the way you're acting. Stop it!"

Five Myths About Bullies

Myth #1:
Bullies have low self-esteem, which is why they pick on other people.

Fact: Some studies have shown that many bullies actually have *high* self-esteem. But they want to feel even *more* powerful and in control.

Myth #2:
Only boys are bullies.

Fact: Girls bully, too. Girl bullies will sometimes pick on boys, and boy bullies will sometimes pick on girls.

Myth #3:

Getting bullied is a normal part of growing up.

Fact: What's "normal" about feeling afraid to go to school? Or putting up with threats or physical abuse? This myth is just an excuse for bad behavior. Plus it helps to create a "code of silence" about bullying. If you think bullying is "normal," you don't say anything about it, and you don't do anything about it. Nobody else does, either. Meanwhile, bullies keep on bullying.

Myth #4:
The best way to handle a bully is by getting even or fighting back.

Fact: Sometimes bullying is a life-or-death situation. If you try to get even with a bully or defend yourself using physical force or a weapon, things will only get worse. Bullies who feel cornered or provoked are likely to come after you again. If a weapon is involved, *you* may be the one who ends up getting hurt.

Myth #5:

If you ignore them, bullies will go away.

Fact: Some bullies may get *more* angry if you ignore them (after all, bullying can be their way of getting attention). They may keep provoking you just to get some kind of reaction.

So, what in the world are you supposed to do when confronted by a bully? Take a deep breath, look the bully in the eye, and say in your firmest, most confident voice:

- "Don't do that. I don't like it," or
- "Leave me alone, I don't like what you're doing," or
- "I'll report you if you don't stop bothering me."

Then walk away.

Because it isn't easy to communicate with a bully, you might want to rehearse what you'll say. At home, stand in front of a mirror and pretend you're talking to the bully. Speak clearly and firmly. Stand tall and show confidence. Practice saying the words until you feel sure of yourself.

You can even ask a family member or friend to help you out by role-playing. That person would play the bully, and you would play yourself. You'll soon get comfortable looking someone in the eye and telling the person to leave you alone.

If the bully keeps bothering you, remember this advice: **WHEN IN DOUBT, SHOUT!** You can yell, "Take your hands off me!" or "You're hurting me!" or "Leave me alone!" Shouting will probably take the bully by surprise, and you'll have a chance to quickly walk away. If you're in a crowded place, other people will most likely turn and look. This may make the bully feel uncomfortable, and he may decide to go away.

Don't be afraid to tell an adult if you're being bullied. You might feel more comfortable talking to the person in private, so the bully can't see or hear you. You are **NOT** a tattletale if you report someone who's hurting you. Here are some adults who can help you: your parents or a relative, your teacher, a school counselor, your principal, or a police officer.

By reporting a bully, you're helping yourself *and* others. Think of all the other kids the bully picks on each day. They'll be grateful that you put a stop to the problem. And believe it or not, you might actually help the bully! With some guidance, bullies can learn to make friends and solve their problems without using violence and intimidation.

Ask your teacher to hold a bully workshop. During the workshop, the class can talk about what bullying is, what causes it, and how to stop it. You could also suggest role-playing exercises, with some students acting as bullies and others as victims. Practice the different strategies for dealing with a bully. It can be very helpful to deal with bully problems in a group setting.

Does your school have a peer mediation program? A mediator, or go-between, might be able to help a bully and victim to make peace. (If the problem is too serious, however, adult help is needed.)

T he benefit of bringing bully problems out in the open is that the bully is no longer in control. It won't be as easy for him to pick on you or other students because everyone will have a better understanding of how to make him stop. And when teachers and school officials are aware of bully problems, they can find ways to help the bully change his behavior.

Do's and Don'ts
for Dealing with Bullies

When a bully teases you about your looks, your clothes, your grades, or anything else . . .

DO stick up for yourself. Say, "You can think what you want. But I'm happy with the way I am." Or, "You have your opinion, I have mine." Or, "Hmmmm . . . thanks for the advice. I'll consider it." Try not to take it personally. The teasing doesn't really have anything to do with *you*. It has to do with the bully's need for power and control.

DON'T begin to gag and gasp for air, clutch your throat and make gurgling noises, fall to the floor choking—and then, when the bully asks what's wrong with you, tell her she's irritating you to death. If you try this crazy stunt, you'll only make things worse. Taunting a bully back is like teasing a vicious dog. (You might end up sitting on an ice pack to soothe the spot where the dog nipped your behind.)

When a bully threatens you . . .

DO use your best judgment and follow your instincts. For example: If a bully says he'll punch your lights out if you don't give him your lunch money, you might say, "I don't want to give you my money. And if you try to force me, I'll report you to the principal." But what if you and the bully are the only two people in the hallway and you're about to get beat up? Give him your money. Then tell an adult.

DON'T drop to your knees and whine, "Here, take my lunch money! Take all of it! Take my backpack, too! I'll do anything you want . . . just don't hurt me! Please, please, please!" Bullies love it when their victims beg for mercy. It makes them want to come back for more.

When a bully calls you names . . .

DO refuse to believe it. Cover your ears and walk away (even whistle the National Anthem to block out the bully's noise). No matter what a bully says, you're not a dork, wimp, teacher's pet, dummy, loser, crybaby, jerk-face, or knucklehead. And anything a bully says about your race, family, gender, or national heritage simply isn't true.

DON'T break down in tears, think "I really *am* a loser," go home and pull the bed covers over your head, stop spending time with your friends, or lose interest in your hobbies because you think you're no good. Remember, bullies love to get under your skin. If you let their mean words hurt you, you'll be giving them what they want.

When a bully picks a fight with you . . .

DO get away as fast as you can, and tell an adult. Tell your teacher, your mom or dad, your principal, or another adult nearby. It takes two to fight. If you refuse to take part, you're less likely to get hurt.

DON'T put up your dukes and say, "I could beat you up with one hand tied behind my back." (This is an invitation to give the tooth fairy a lot of work.) If you get into a fight, you have nothing to gain and everything to lose. Chances are, the bully has had a lot more practice using her fists. And if you get caught fighting on school grounds, both of you will get into trouble, no matter who started it.

When you see a bully coming toward you . . .

DO get out of his way! Step aside, join your friends, strike up a conversation with someone nearby, or walk toward a crowded place. This way, the bully can't get you alone.

DON'T pick your nose and pretend you're about to eat it, in the hope that the bully will throw up with disgust and leave you in peace.

*D*id you know that many bullies are budding actors? They spend a lot of time rehearsing their clever lines, such as "I'm going to teach you a lesson you'll never forget," "You're dead, kid," and "I'm gonna rearrange your face." You'd think they were up for Academy Awards!

Learning self-defense is a good way to protect yourself and increase your self-confidence. You might try taking a karate class. In karate, you'll find out how to defend yourself, and you'll gain the confidence *not* to fight. (And, if you wear your black belt to school, bullies will get the message!)

Sometimes humor can help ease a conflict. If a bully threatens to beat you up, you might say, "Hey, I'll save you the time and trouble. I'll go home right now and beat myself up. That way, your hands won't get hurt." The bully may laugh and decide to leave you alone. (**CAUTION:** Be sure your joke isn't directed at the bully. He might think you're making fun of him.)

Sometimes an "I-message" can cool a bully down. For example: If a bully calls you a big dork, don't say, "You're mean when you call me that!" Say, "I don't like it when you call me that, because it really annoys me. Besides, I am **NOT** a big dork, as anyone can plainly see." A "you-message" puts the other person on the defensive. An "I-message" says what you feel.

Want to surprise a bully? Try making friends with him! Bullies have trouble making friends and getting along with others, so they seek attention by becoming the toughest, meanest kids in school. Set a good example for the bully by acting like a friend. You and other students might be able to change a bully's behavior this way.

Are <u>You</u> a Bully?

Are you wondering if you're a bully? Here's a quick way to tell. Look over the following list. If you answer "yes" to one or two of these questions, you may be on your way to becoming a bully. If you answer "yes" to three or more of these questions, you probably *are* a bully and you need to find ways to change your behavior.

1. Do you pick on people who are smaller than you, or on animals?
2. Do you like to tease and taunt other people?
3. If you tease people, do you like to see them get upset?
4. Do you think it's funny when other people make mistakes?

5. Do you like to take or destroy other people's belongings?

6. Do you want other students to think you're the toughest kid in school?

7. Do you get angry a lot and stay angry for a long time?

8. Do you blame other people for things that go wrong in your life?

9. Do you like to get revenge on people who hurt you?

10. When you play a game or sport, do you always have to be the winner?

11. If you lose at something, do you worry about what other people will think of you?

12. Do you get angry or jealous when someone else succeeds?

Uh-oh! Did you just find out that you're a bully? Or maybe the list describes someone else you know—your big brother or sister, or your best friend.

The good news is: Bullies can get help dealing with their feelings, getting along with other people, and making friends. Parents, teachers, school counselors, and other adults can all give this kind of help. Just ask.

One thing bullies and their victims have in common is **ANGER.** Bullies take their anger out on their victims, and their victims feel angry because of the way the bullies treat them.

The next time anger boils up inside you, try dealing with it positively. Take a few deep breaths, count backwards until you feel more relaxed, imagine a peaceful place, pet your cat, think about things that make you feel good, or go and talk to someone about your anger.

Everybody, everywhere has been bullied at some point in their lives. Even the bullies of the world have been bullied! (Which is one reason why they act the way they do.) But that doesn't mean bullying is OK. Or that you should suffer in silence. Or that you should be a bully yourself.

What will *you* do the next time someone bullies you?

Think about it. Make a plan. Be ready to speak up, walk away, or run away.

Bullies are a pain in the brain. But they don't have to give *you* a permanent headache.

A Message to Teachers and Parents

Newspapers and magazines are filled with stories about violent incidents occurring in schools across the country. You've probably read about gangs, students bringing guns to school, fights that get out of control, and sexual harassment. At the root of this violence is a widespread but often overlooked problem: bullying.

Most of us can recall a time when we've been bullied. But today bullying is more serious. Kids have taken desperate measures, such as using a gun in self-defense or committing suicide, to deal with their bully problem. Many children are afraid to go to school. While at school, they avoid areas perceived as dangerous, such as rest rooms and secluded hallways.

Many school officials are now becoming more aware of how serious and widespread bullying is. In some schools, antiviolence and conflict-resolution programs are helping bullies and their victims find ways to get along. It's important to implement system-wide efforts and strategies to continue to curb bullying. For example, victims need to feel confident that if they report a bullying problem to school officials, something will be done. And bullies need to understand that their behavior won't be tolerated.

If you're a teacher, you can take steps to curb bullying in your classroom and beyond:

1. Find out how common bullying is in your school. Create and distribute an anonymous questionnaire, or talk privately with other teachers, your students, and their parents.

2. Set firm rules against bullying in your classroom.

3. Be aware of incidents of aggression that take place in the bathrooms, on the playground, in the lunchroom, and in hallways. Monitor these areas to ensure a safer school environment.

4. Keep a written record of bullying incidents, including the names, dates, times, and circumstances. Submit the reports to the principal.

5. Give students a chance to talk about bullying and its effects. Hold workshops or class discussions.

6. Get administrators and parents involved in reinforcing good behavior and supporting victims of bullying.

If you're a parent, you may not be aware that your child is being bullied. Many kids are afraid to let an adult know what's happening. They feel embarrassed and think they have to handle the situation on their own. Have you noticed any of the following signs in your child?

- Skips school or is often too sick to go to school,
- Has unexplained bruises,
- Has experienced a slip in grades,
- Is reluctant to talk about school,
- Is missing belongings,
- Frequently requests lunch money to replace "lost" money,
- Comes home in dirty clothes (from fights).

If you see a few or several of these signs, your child might be having trouble with a bully.

Here's what you can do if your child is being bullied:

1. Talk with your child, letting him or her know that you understand and care.

2. Get in touch with your child's teacher or with school officials to inform them of the situation. Do this after school, by phone, or in a letter to protect your child's privacy and to make sure that the bully or other kids don't find out. Keep written accounts of the bullying incidents and the times when you've talked with school staff members about the problem.

3. Teach your child the skills needed to resolve a bully situation. Throughout this book, you'll find several ideas you can role-play and practice with your child. "Fighting back" or "ignoring the bully" isn't the solution. Instead, your child needs to be verbally assertive and have the confidence to seek the help of an adult.

If you suspect that your child is the one doing the bullying, try some of these options:

- Talk to your child about the reasons behind the bullying. Reassure your child that you still love him or her.
- Consider family counseling to determine the cause of the problem. Your child may need help learning to manage anger and to resolve conflicts peacefully.
- Help your child understand the differences between aggressive and assertive behaviors.
- Let your child's teacher know that your child is trying to stop bullying. The teacher may be helpful in setting goals and correcting bad behavior.

On pages 95–104 are lists of resources that can help you learn more about bullies and what to do about them. Share these resources with your students or your child, and work together to find solutions to the problem of bullying. Help your children to help themselves!

Resources for Students

Books

The Bully of Barkham Street by Mary Stolz (NY: Harper & Row, 1963). In this humorous and touching fictional story about eleven-year-old bully Martin Hastings, you'll learn what life can be like from a bully's point of view. Ages 9–13.

Dealing with Bullying by Marianne Johnston (NY: Rosen, 1996). This book describes what is meant by bullying, then explains why bullies act the way they do, how to deal with them, and how to stop being one. Ages 10–12.

How to Handle Bullies, Teasers and Other Meanies: A Book That Takes the Nuisance Out of Name Calling and Other Nonsense by Kate Cohen-Posey (Highland City, FL: Rainbow Books, Inc., 1995). This book talks about name calling, prejudice, anger, and dangerous situations. It also explains how people become bullies and teasers. You'll find ideas for melting meanness, healthy ways to respond to insults and teasing, and suggestions for turning negative situations into positive ones. There are even ideas that will help a parent or teacher to help you. Ages 9–14.

Stick Boy by Joan T. Zeier (NY: Atheneum, 1993). A fictional story about sixth grader Eric Bonner, who survives his parents' divorce, moving to a new state, and going to a new school, where he is teased and tormented by a bully who calls him "Stick Boy." Ages 9–13.

Stick Up for Yourself: Every Kid's Guide to Personal Power and Positive Self-Esteem by Gershen Kaufman, Ph.D., and Lev Raphael, Ph.D. (Minneapolis: Free Spirit Publishing Inc., 1990). This book tells you how to stick up for yourself with other kids, big sisters and brothers, even parents and teachers. It can help you feel better about yourself, stronger inside, and more in charge of your life. Ages 8–12.

Why Is Everybody Always Picking On Me? A Guide to Handling Bullies by Terrence Webster-Doyle (Middlebury, VT: Atrium Society Education for Peace Publications, 1991). Find out how to cope with bullies, understand why bullies do what they do, and gain the confidence to win without fighting. This book is filled with creative stories and activities on resolving conflicts without harm. Ages 10–18.

Veronica Ganz by Marilyn Sachs (Garden City, NY: Doubleday & Company, Inc., 1968). In this fictional story, Veronica Ganz is tormented by the new kid in class, Peter Wedemeyer. Her strategies for stopping him fail again and again, until one day she tries something new—and discovers the "weapon" she's been looking for is something she's had all along. Ages 10–13.

Organizations

I Don't Care Club
c/o Rachel Bradley
420 Strickland Street
Glastonbury, CT 06033

Rachel Bradley, 15, knows what it's like to be teased and bullied. Kids at her school taunted her repeatedly, so she decided to start a club for other young people in her situation. "I Don't Care" means members don't care what others think of them—they are proud of their individuality and won't stand for teasing anymore. Rachel's club has drawn a lot of publicity on TV and in magazines and newspapers. While the club no longer holds regular meetings, Rachel still wants to be a resource for kids dealing with bully situations. She encourages you to write to her about your problems, and she'll write back. Rachel can give you information on starting your own local "I Don't Care" club.

National Crime Prevention Council
1700 K Street, NW
Second Floor
Washington, D.C. 20006-3817
(202) 466-6272
http://www.weprevent.org

This nonprofit organization works to help people prevent crime and build safer, more caring communities. Take a look at their Web site, which has information on McGruff houses.

Web site

kidscape
http://www.solnet.co.uk/kidscape/kids4.htm

At this site, kids can find a page called *You Can Beat Bullying—A Guide for Young People,* with tons of interesting information about bullies. Find out what makes some people become bullies, what to do if you're having bully problems, how to get help, and much more. Young people who have been bullied or have been bullies share what they went through, how their lives changed, and what they think about it now. There's also a page at this site called *Preventing Bullying—A Parent's Guide.* Share it with a parent!

Resources for Teachers and Parents

Books

Bullies & Victims: Helping Your Child through the School-yard Battlefield by SuEllen Fried and Paula Fried, Ph.D. (NY: M. Evans and Company, Inc., 1996). This guide alerts parents and children to the differences between normal peer teasing and bullying situations; helps parents, teachers, and counselors understand the dynamics and act effectively when children are bullying or being bullied; and offers practical steps to help children prevent and solve the problem.

Bullying at School: What We Know and What We Can Do by Dan Olweus (Cambridge, MA: Blackwell Publishers, 1993). A book for parents, teachers, and school principals. Explains the causes and consequences of bullying, tells how to recognize if a child is being victimized or is bullying others, and details effective ways of counteracting and preventing bullying problems.

Good Friends Are Hard to Find: Help Your Child Find, Make, and Keep Friends by Fred Frankel, Ph.D. (Pasadena, CA: Perspective Publishing, 1996). Step-by-step advice to help parents help their kids (ages 5–12) to find, make, and keep friends; solve problems with other kids; and deal with teasing, bullying, meanness, and stormy relationships.

The Safe Child Book by Sherryll Kraizer, Ph.D. (NY: Fireside, 1996). This book gives parents effective and nonthreatening techniques for teaching children how to protect themselves without making them afraid. It addresses abuse and school safety, and suggests ways to build self-esteem and lifeskills.

Organizations

Committee for Children
2203 Airport Way South, Suite 500
Seattle, WA 98134
1-800-634-4449

Offers information, a curriculum, and videos addressing violence prevention, impulse control, and conflict resolution, for use at home or in K–8 classrooms. Call or write for a free list of products and services.

Juvenile Justice Clearinghouse
P.O. Box 6000
Rockville, MD 20849
1-800-638-8736

This component of the National Criminal Justice Reference Service offers materials addressing juvenile justice, crime prevention, violence prevention, children's rights, and more. Call or write to request a list of available materials.

National School Safety Center
4165 Thousand Oaks Blvd., Suite 290
Westlake Village, CA 91362
(805) 373-9977

Offers helpful booklets and videos addressing violence prevention, bullying, and conflict resolution for educators and parents. Call or write to request a free catalog.

Web sites

Disney's Family Site
http://www.family.com

An entertaining, informative, helpful site for kids,
parents, and anyone who cares a lot about young
people. When you visit, you'll find advice from
experts in medicine, law, and child care; information
on hot news topics; ideas for fun, creative things to
do with your family; chat rooms where you can share
experiences with and get helpful hints and advice
from other kids and parents; and much more.
Especially useful is the site's extensive archive of
articles and features on various parenting topics—
you can search by a keyword for tips on dealing with
bullies, safety in school, and helping kids stick up for
themselves.

The Safe Child Home Page
http://safechild.org

This site has loads of helpful information and practical ideas addressing issues like preventing abuse, teaching safety, developing lifeskills, and managing risk. Check out the area devoted to bullies, where parents and educators can find information on dealing with bullies; why people become bullies; what to do if your child is being bullied; what to do if your child *is* the bully; how to prevent bully problems; and much more. Sponsored by Coalition for Children. Coalition Director Sherryll Kraizer, Ph.D., is the author of *The Safe Child Book* (see page 101).

About the Author/Illustrator

When South African-born Trevor Romain was 12, his teacher told him he wasn't talented enough to do art. By accident, he found out 20 years later that he could draw. Since that lucky day, he has written and illustrated 13 books for children, including *How To Do Homework Without Throwing Up* (Free Spirit Publishing). In addition to writing, illustrating, drinking tea, and trying to avoid trouble, Trevor regularly visits schools to speak to children, and he spends his free time with kids who have cancer at the Brackenridge Hospital in Austin, Texas. He has spoken to almost 40,000 children over the last five years and has had over 100 articles written about his work enriching children's lives. Trevor receives hundreds of letters annually from principals, teachers, and students who have been touched by his humor and energy.

OTHER GREAT BOOKS FROM FREE SPIRIT!

How To Do Homework Without Throwing Up
written and illustrated by Trevor Romain

Hilarious cartoons and witty insights teach important tru
about homework and positive, practical strategies for get
it done. For ages 8–13.

72 pp., illust., s/c, 5⅛" x 7", ISBN 1-57542-011-2, $8.95

Stick Up for Yourself!
Every Kid's Guide to Personal Power and Positive Se
Esteem

by Gershen Kaufman, Ph.D., and Lev Raphael, Ph.D.

Realistic, encouraging how-to advice for kids on being
assertive, building relationships, and becoming respon
For ages 8–12.

96 pp., illust., s/c, 6" x 9", ISBN 0-915793-17-2, $9.95

Stick Up for Yourself! Teacher's Guide
A 10-Part Course in Self-Esteem and Assertiveness
Kids

*by Gerri Johnson, Gershen Kaufman, Ph.D., and
Lev Raphael, Ph.D.*

Includes 14 reproducible handout masters. For teache
grades 3–7.

128 pp., 8½ x 11, ISBN 0-915793-31-8, $18.95

To place an order or request our free catalog,
please write, call, email, or visit our Web site:

Free Spirit Publishing Inc.
400 First Avenue North • Suite 616 • Minneapolis, MN 55401-1730
call toll-free 800.735.7323 • or locally 612.338.2068
help4kids@freespirit.com • www.freespirit.com